MONTH-BY-MONTH POCKET CHARTS

**20 Knock-Your-Socks-Off Pocket Chart Poems With Lessons
That Take You Through the Year & Build Skills in Reading,
Math, Science & More**

By Valerie SchifferDanoff

SCHOLASTIC
PROFESSIONAL BOOKS

New York ❋ Toronto ❋ London ❋ Auckland

Sydney ❋ Mexico City ❋ New Delhi ❋ Hong Kong

Dedication

Dedicated to the memory of my father, Michael Schiffer, for his ninety-one plus years
of hopes, dreams, inspiration, and encouragement.
December 25, 1908? – January 29, 1999

Credits

"School Bus" by Kay Winters, illustrated by Martha Weston. From DID YOU SEE WHAT I
SAW? by Kay Winters, copyright © 1996 by Kay Winters. Used by permission of Viking
Penguin, an imprint of Penguin Putnam Books for Young Readers, a division of Penguin
Putnam, Inc.

"Five Little Monsters" by Eve Merriam. From BLACKBERRY INK by Eve Merriam. (A
Mulberry Paperback) Copyright © 1985 by Eve Merriam. Used by permission of Marian
Reiner.

"Sudden Storm" by Elizabeth Coatsworth. From THE SPARROW BUSH by Elizabeth
Coatsworth. Copyright © 1966 by Elizabeth Coatsworth.

"June is a Tune" by Sarah Wilson. From JUNE IS A TUNE THAT JUMPS ON A STAIR by
Sarah Wilson. Copyright © 1992 Sarah Wilson. Reprinted by permission of the author.

"Happy Chinese New Year" and "Eggs on Me" by Helen H. Moore. Reprinted by permission of
the author.

Cover design by Norma Ortiz
Cover photographs by Donnelly Marks
Interior design by Russell Cohen
Interior photographs by Valerie SchifferDanoff
Interior illustrations by Rusty Fletcher

ISBN 0-439-07350-2
Copyright © 2001 by Valerie SchifferDanoff
All rights reserved.
Printed in the U.S.A.

TABLE OF CONTENTS

INTRODUCTION

Pocket charts are perfect for introducing a wide variety of topics to your class. In this book you'll find pocket charts chock-full of rich teaching opportunities and fun activities that will take you through the entire school year.

Each month, you'll find two fresh ideas for pocket charts that support your curriculum. Children follow directions as they construct a rake for fall, learn about the life cycle of a pumpkin, celebrate other cultures' winter holidays, count by tens for the 100th Day of School, and much more! Kid-pleasing art templates liven up pocket charts and can be used to match words with pictures, help children count objects, or support the text. Easy, step-by-step instructions show how to set up each pocket chart and how to use it as a versatile teaching tool.

DISPLAYING POCKET CHARTS

Pocket charts can be used anytime, anywhere in the classroom. Use them for whole-class instruction during circle time, small-group lessons, or in independent, hands-on learning centers.

You can display pocket charts on a bulletin board, secured by heavy-duty pushpins, or on an easel with easel clips. You can also use heavy-duty Velcro to hang pocket charts on walls or from shelves. Pocket chart stands also are available at teaching supply stores and through mail-order catalogs.

Some pocket charts tend to roll inward when suspended. You may want to place a thin dowel, cut to the width of the chart, in the bottom pocket behind the sentence strip. Dowels can be purchased at hardware stores, home stores, or craft shops, and then cut to size.

When hanging up a pocket chart for young learners, put it at the children's eye level so they can easily reach into a pocket to add to or change the sentence strips.

SIZES OF POCKET CHARTS AND SENTENCE STRIPS

Pocket charts come in a variety of sizes and colors, as do sentence strips. The typical pocket chart is 34- by 42-inches with ten pockets. For smaller spaces in the classroom, a 24- by 24-inch chart is also available. The most versatile size is 42- by 58-inches. It has ten pockets but twice as much space because of its width. Display two activities simultaneously by dividing the chart with a piece of colored masking tape or by hanging blank sentence strips vertically.

Pocket charts are usually manufactured in blue. However, the Teaching Resource Center Catalog (1-800-833-3389) offer charts in red, pink, lavender, yellow, green, and white.

The best sentence strips for use in pocket charts are of tag-quality paper, precut to 3- by 24-inches. These are available in white, beige, and packs of assorted pastel colors. Sentence strips also come in less-expensive rolls, but the money you save may not be worth the aggravation of straightening them out. If you can purchase several different colors, you can use them in many ways. For example, you can write rhyming lines on the same-color strips to highlight the rhymes, or write color names on matching strips. Throughout this book, optional color choices are given. But keep in mind that the lessons will still work wonderfully if you use only one color.

STORING SENTENCE STRIPS

You can store sentence strips by theme, skill, or concept. Keep them in a flat folder made by folding a large piece of cardboard in half. A butterfly clip, large paper clip, or small clamp holds each set of strips together.

Here are other ways to store sentence strips:
- long-stem flower box, which most florists stock
- wallpaper glue holder
- cardboard wallpaper box, cut along the top
- box in which the sentence strips arrived, covered with contact paper
- two manila folders, opened, folded length-wise and attached with tape

TEACHING TECHNIQUES FOR POCKET CHARTS

When using pocket charts in the early childhood classroom, take into consideration the development and experience of your children. A kindergarten student may never have seen a pocket chart before, so you may want to demonstrate the basic steps to follow in a lesson. Here are some tips to keep in mind when teaching with pocket charts:

- Write entire words or sentences on sentence strips and then cut them apart. These can then be arranged in the appropriate pockets of the chart. (Note: Keeping the rhythmic structure of a poem can sometimes be difficult when copying and placing a poem in the chart. You may want to space the words in the chart so children can see where to pause between words.)

- Model how to use the components in the pocket chart. Teach children how to place words, sentence strips, and templates in the pocket chart and how to carefully remove them.

- When reading from a pocket chart, encourage children to read with you. Read through the poem once and then again with the children, pointing to each word as you read.

- When teaching a short poem, chant or repeat the poem to the natural rhythm that occurs. You will find that the class will establish a rhythm. Children love to chant sets of rhyming words.

- When brainstorming ideas during a pocket chart lesson, encourage everyone to participate.

- Use pictures in addition to or instead of words. This allows children to match words to pictures and pictures to words.

- Use cutouts or stickers as manipulative materials.

These ideas are just for starters. Use your imagination and the imaginations of your students to come up with new uses for pocket charts, lessons, and follow-up activities. Also, see how many more titles you can add to the literature links!

RESOURCES FOR POCKET CHART SUPPLIES

The basic materials you need to complete the lessons in this book are available at most teaching supply stores. You can also get them through the companies listed below:

- Teaching Resource Center Catalog (1-800-833-3389)
- American Academic Supplies (1-800-325-9118)
- Beckley-Cardy (1-800-227-1178)

MORE RESOURCES FOR POEMS

When choosing poems, look for those with simple language and uncomplicated text. Avoid too much symbolism. Short rhyming poems are best.

Scholastic Integrated Language Arts Resource Book by Valerie SchifferDanoff
(Scholastic, 1995)

The Pocket Chart Book by Valerie SchifferDanoff
(Scholastic, 1996)

Pocket Charts for Emergent Readers by Valerie SchifferDanoff
(Scholastic, 1997)

15 Pocket Charts for Math by Valerie SchifferDanoff
(Scholastic, 1999)

Poetry Place Anthology
(Scholastic, 1983)

Thematic Poems, Songs, and Fingerplays by Meish Goldish
(Scholastic, 1994)

The Random House Book of Poetry selected by Jack Prelutsky
(Random House, 1983)

Read-Aloud Rhymes for the Very Young selected by Jack Prelutsky
(Alfred A. Knopf, 1986)

You Be Good & I'll Be Night by Eve Merriam
(Mulberry Books, 1996)

SEPTEMBER

Welcome students back to school with a catchy poem that gets them moving.
Then, greet fall with a colorful project that's sure to brighten your room.

SCHOOL BUS

PURPOSE

Children distinguish between the concepts of size, speed, on, off, open, and shut, while they burn off some of that early school year energy.

POCKET CHART POEM

> **School Bus by Kay Winters**
>
> **OUR BUS**
>
> **is a   BIG**
>
> **Bright   Loud   Bumpy**
>
> **STOP and start**
>
> **Fast and s l o w**
>
> **On and off   Open—shut**
>
> **Yellow box**
>
> **on wheels.**
>
> **Stuffed with kids!**

MATERIALS

* 34- by 42-inch pocket chart
* 14 yellow sentence strips
* school bus template (page 14)
* card stock
* colored markers
* scissors

SETTING UP

1. Write each line of the poem on a separate sentence strip, as shown.
2. Copy the school bus template on card stock in at least three different sizes. Color the buses and cut them out. You may want to trace one bus on solid yellow paper, for the line "Yellow box."
3. Place one bus, the title, and the first line, "OUR BUS," in the chart.

TEACHING WITH THE POCKET CHART

1. Invite the children to sit in front of the chart. Tell them that you have a poem about a school bus.
2. Ask the children to think about words that describe a school bus, such as its color and size. If they call out any words in the poem, such as *big* and *yellow*, place these words in the appropriate pockets in the chart.
3. Encourage children to describe how it feels to ride on the bus. If they call out *loud* or *bumpy*, place these words in the

chart as well.

4. Next, ask the children how the bus moves. Insert *fast*, *slow*, *stop*, and *start* in the chart as children call them out.

5. Once these words are in place, put the rest of the words in the chart and read the poem with the children.

6. Ask, "Why do you think the author calls the bus 'a yellow box'?" This will help them identify shape and introduce them to the concept of *allusion*—when an author refers to something indirectly by describing its properties.

FOLLOW-UP ACTIVITIES

* Discuss opposite concepts in the poem: on and off, open and shut, fast and slow, stop and start. Invite the children to look around the room and ask them, "What else can be off or on?" (*Lights*) "What else can be open or shut?" (*Doors*)

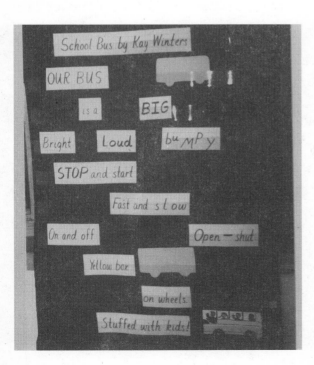

* Have children set the poem to actions. For instance, they can bounce up and down on their seats to act out the word *bumpy*; move fast and then slow; open and shut their hands to imitate the motion of the doors.

LITERATURE LINKS

The Wheels on the Bus by Maryann Kovalski (Little Brown & Co., 1990)

The Wheels on the Bus by Paul Zelinsky (Penguin Putnam, 2000)

SEPTEMBER

RAKE THE LEAVES

PURPOSE

Children read a rebus and use visual cues to follow directions and make their own rakes.

POCKET CHART WORDS

Rake the Leaves

1. Trace and cut a yellow rake.

2. Trace and cut a blue handle.

Glue the handle to the rake.

3. Trace and cut one green leaf,

one orange leaf, one purple leaf,

one red leaf, and one brown leaf.

4. Glue the five leaves to the rake.

MATERIALS

* 34- by 42-inch pocket chart
* 3 white sentence strips
* 2 blue sentence strips
* 1 sentence strip each in yellow, green, purple, red (or pink), orange, and brown
* rake and leaf templates (pages 15–17)
* colored markers
* card stock

* yellow, blue, green, purple, red (or pink), orange, and brown construction paper for each child
* scissors
* glue

SETTING UP

1. Copy the title, the words "Trace and cut," and the last line of directions on white sentence strips. Write the first line on a yellow strip and both sentences of the second line on blue. Write the different colored leaves on matching sentence strips. (Or use colored markers that correspond to the leaf colors.)

2. Draw a simple triangle above the word *rake* on the first line. Draw a straight line above *handle* on the second line. Write the symbol for each number above the number words.

3. Copy the leaf templates on card stock and cut them out. Write the word *leaf* on each one.

4. Copy the rake handle and the head of the rake on card stock. Cut out the pieces and label as *handle* and *rake*.

5. Insert the directions and templates in the

chart. Attach an assembled rake complete with each color leaf to the chart using an easel clip or butterfly clip.

6. Place additional construction paper near the chart for children to use.

TEACHING WITH THE POCKET CHART

1. Engage children in a discussion about the different colors of leaves they can see outside now. Ask, "Have you ever helped your parents rake leaves?" Tell children that they will be making a rake by following the directions on the pocket chart.

2. Read the directions with the children. Pause at each color and have children take turns coming up to the chart to point to the corresponding leaf color on the finished rake.

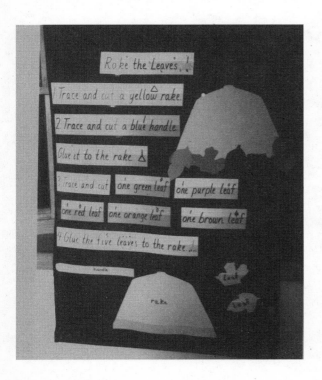

3. Demonstrate to children how to use the templates. Trace each piece onto construction paper and cut the shape.

4. Show children how to assemble their rakes and attach the leaves using glue.

NOTE: This can be an independent activity or an assisted small-group activity, depending on the children's ages. The finished rakes also make a great bulletin-board display.

FOLLOW-UP ACTIVITIES

* Have children write the colors on their finished projects.

* Write a poem about colors to display on the rakes. Brainstorm words to fit this pattern:

> Fall is as red as . . .
> Fall is as green as . . .
> Fall is as purple as . . .

A finished poem may look like this:

> Fall is as red as an apple.
> Fall is as green as a leaf.
> Fall is as purple as a grape.

LITERATURE LINKS

Red Leaf, Yellow Leaf by Lois Ehlert (Harcourt, Brace, Jovanovich, 1991)

Why Do Leaves Change Color? by Betsy Maestro (HarperTrophy, 1994)

SCHOOL BUS TEMPLATE

RAKE THE LEAVES TEMPLATES

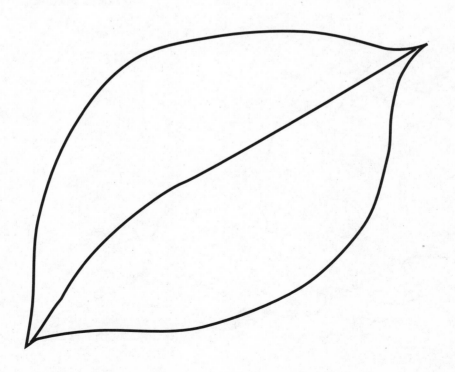

RAKE THE LEAVES TEMPLATES

RAKE HANDLE

RAKE THE LEAVES TEMPLATE

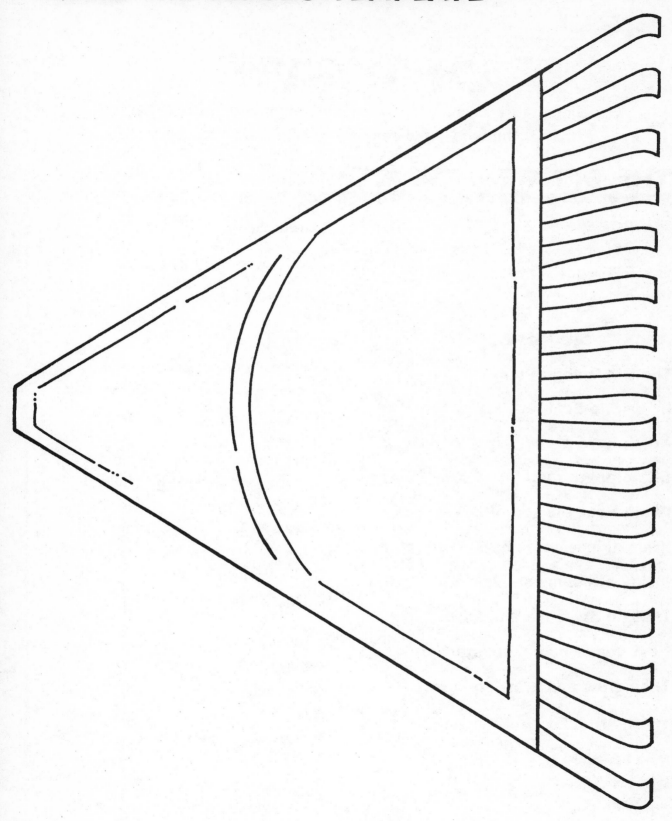

OCTOBER

Get ready for tricks and treats! Pumpkins and monsters are in the air.
Invite them into your classroom with these October charts.

THE BIG ORANGE PUMPKIN

PURPOSE

Children learn about seeds and the growing process. They also learn to recognize rhyming words.

POCKET CHART POEM

The Big Orange Pumpkin

by Valerie Schiffer

Now I have a pumpkin

Big, orange, round, and fat.

When I cut the top off,

It looks just like a hat.

Inside are slimy seeds

That I'll dry, save and sow.

Next year's pumpkins start small

Then grow and grow and grow.

MATERIALS

* 34- by 42-inch pocket chart
* 9 orange sentence strips
* 1 yellow and 1 green sentence strip
* pumpkin and seeds templates (page 23)

* colored markers
* card stock
* scissors
* a real pumpkin (optional)

SETTING UP

1. Copy the poem on sentence strips, writing the words *fat* and *hat* on yellow sentence strips, and *sow* and *grow* on green.
2. Copy the pumpkin template on card stock in four different sizes. Color the smallest pumpkin green and the other three pumpkins orange. Cut them out.
3. Copy the seeds template on card stock and color it green. Cut it out.
4. Place the first line in the chart.

TEACHING WITH THE POCKET CHART

1. Show children the largest pumpkin template. Ask them to describe the pumpkin. As they suggest the words *big, orange, round,* and *fat*, place the corresponding sentence strip in the appropriate pocket.
2. Ask, "What do we usually do with a pumpkin at this time of year?" (*Children may offer responses such as carve it,*

decorate it, or draw on it.) Explain that a pumpkin that has a face drawn or carved on it is called a jack-o'-lantern.

3. Ask, "What is one of the first things we do to turn a pumpkin into a jack-o'-lantern?" The response you're looking for is in the next line of the poem ("When I cut the top off,..."). As the children respond, place the line in the pocket.

4. Insert the next line in the poem except for the word *hat*. Ask the children to come up with words that rhyme with *fat*. When they guess the correct word, add it to the chart.

5. Continue by discussing what's inside the pumpkin. Explain that pumpkin seeds can be dried and then planted next spring. Place lines five and six in the chart. Explain that the word *sow* means "to plant."

6. Place line seven in the chart and show the smallest, green pumpkin. Ask children for an appropriate word that rhymes with *sow*. When they guess the word *grow*, insert the rest of the poem.

7. Have the children read the whole poem with you. Explain that for pumpkins to be ready for picking in the fall, their seeds have to be planted in the spring and grow over the summer.

FOLLOW-UP ACTIVITIES

* Invite children to act out the poem as you read it aloud. Have them use their arms to illustrate *big* and *round*. They may move their hand around in a circle as if cutting off the top of the pumpkin. They can touch their heads for a hat. Have them pretend to scoop out and then plant the seeds. To show the different sizes of the pumpkins, have children touch their thumb to their index finger for the smallest pumpkin; form a circle with the fingers of both hands for the next size; cup both hands but slightly spread apart for the next size; and finally, bend their arms out in front of their bodies to indicate the largest pumpkin.

* Bring in a real pumpkin and cut off the top. Invite children to help scoop out the seeds. Then carve out eyes, a nose, and a mouth to make a jack-o'-lantern.

* Sprout some seeds in a plastic bag lined with a paper towel. To do this, fold a paper towel to fit halfway up a self-sealing sandwich bag. Moisten the towel and put

it inside the bag. Staple the towel to the bag about one-half inch from the bottom. Place the seeds above the staples. The seeds should sprout in about two or three days. You can hang the sprouts on the chart with clips.

LITERATURE LINKS

Pumpkin, Pumpkin by Jeanne Titherington (Econo-Clad, 1999)

Apples and Pumpkins by Anne Rockwell (Aladdin, 1994)

The Biggest Pumpkin Ever by Steven Kroll (Scholastic, 1993)

Picking Apples and Pumpkins by Amy and Richard Hutchings (Scholastic, 1994)

Pumpkin Fiesta by Caryn Yocowitz (HarperCollins, 1998)

OCTOBER

FIVE LITTLE MONSTERS

POCKET CHART POEM

Five Little Monsters

by Eve Merriam

Five little monsters

by the light of the moon,

Stirring pudding with

a wooden pudding spoon.

The first one says,

"It mustn't be runny."

The second one says,

"That would make it taste funny."

The third one says,

"It mustn't be lumpy."

The fourth one says,

"That would make me grumpy."

The fifth one smiles,

hums a little tune,

And licks all the drippings

from the wooden pudding spoon.

PURPOSE

Children learn about ordinal numbers and the use of quotation marks.

MATERIALS

* 34- by 42-inch pocket chart
* 8 yellow sentence strips
* 5 orange sentence strips
* monsters and treat bag templates (pages 24–25)
* colored markers
* card stock
* scissors

SETTING UP

1. Copy the part of each sentence in quotes on an orange sentence strip. Write the rest of the sentences on yellow strips.
2. Copy the monster templates on card stock. Color them and cut them out.
3. Make five copies of the treat bag template on card stock. Color them in five different colors and cut them out. Put the treat bags in the bottom pocket of the chart.
4. Place the sentence strips in the pocket chart, leaving space between the phrases and the quoted sentences. Insert the

monster templates before the quoted sentences in the following order: witch, skeleton, dinosaur, clown, and cat.

TEACHING WITH THE POCKET CHART

1. Tell the children you have a poem about five little monsters. Share the poem. Ask, "Who do you think the monsters really are?" *(Children in costumes)*

2. Ask children, "Which is the first monster?" *(Witch)* Call on a volunteer to take a treat bag and place it next to the first monster. Next, ask, "Which is the second monster?" *(Skeleton)* Ask another volunteer to place a treat bag next to the second monster, and so on.

3. Read the poem again, this time changing

your voice as you read the sentences in quotations. Ask, "What's so special about the words in the orange sentence strips?" *(They're the words the monsters are saying.)* Point to the quotation marks around each sentence and explain to children that these marks can be found at the beginning and end of a person's exact words.

FOLLOW-UP ACTIVITIES

* Ask the class to suggest motions for each monster, especially the last one that doesn't speak.

* Invite five children at a time to come up and pretend they are the monsters. If they cannot read yet, coach them with their lines. Encourage them to be expressive. Repeat the process until everyone in the class has had a turn.

LITERATURE LINKS

Halloween Cats by Jean Marzollo (Scholastic, 1992)

One Hungry Monster by Susan Heyboer O'Keefe (Little Brown, 1992)

Seven Little Monsters by Maurice Sendak (HarperCollins, 1987)

THE BIG ORANGE PUMPKIN TEMPLATES

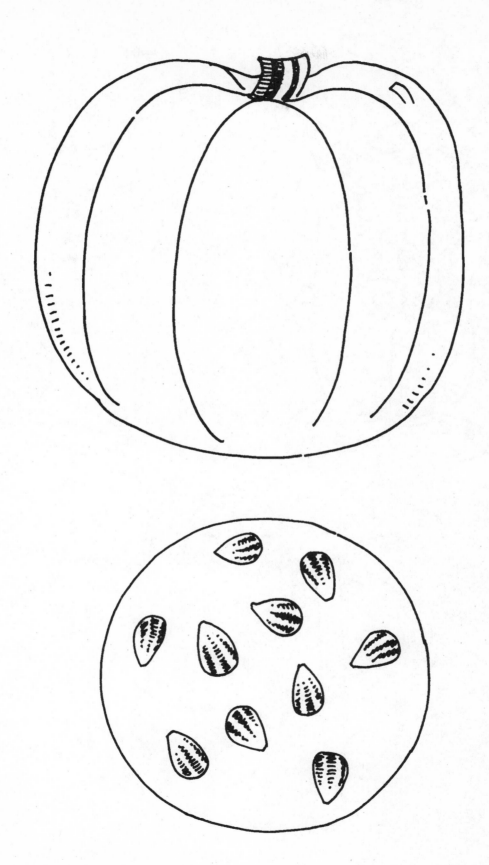

FIVE LITTLE MONSTERS TEMPLATES

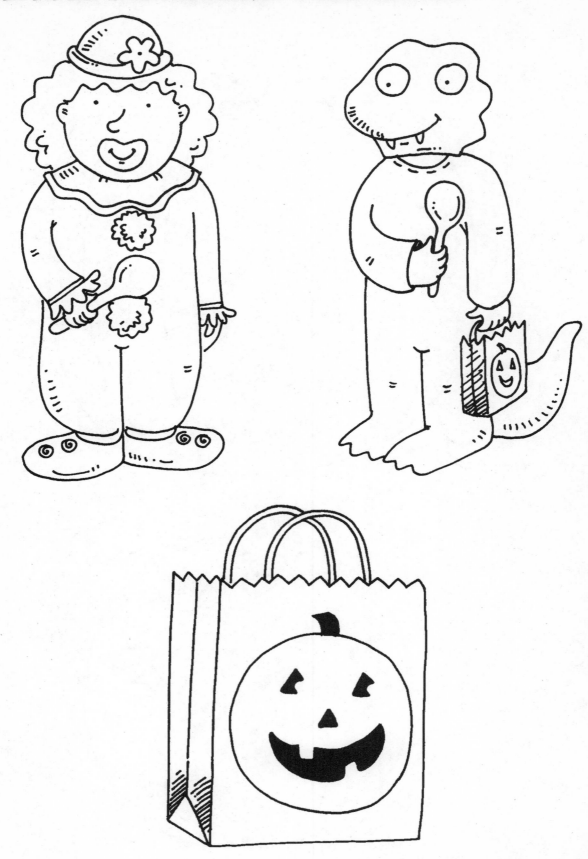

FIVE LITTLE MONSTERS TEMPLATES

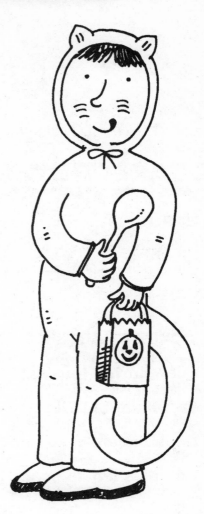

NOVEMBER

Bring the harvest into your classroom with the help of a scarecrow who has finished his work for the season. Then, enjoy the bounty with an inviting table full of Thanksgiving foods.

SCARECROW'S HARVEST

PURPOSE

Children learn the basic concepts of planting and harvesting, and gain an understanding of the seasons.

POCKET CHART POEM

Scarecrow's Harvest

by Valerie Schiffer

Oh, scarecrow, scarecrow

No one's left to scare.

All the corn's been picked.

The ground is very clear.

The harvest is in.

Nothing's 'bout to grow.

Wait till next spring.

And then you'll be

A scary scarecrow!

MATERIALS

* 34- by 42-inch pocket chart
* 10 sentence strips
* scarecrow, corn, cornucopia, and haystack templates (pages 30–31)
* colored markers
* card stock
* scissors

SETTING UP

1. Write each line of the poem on a separate sentence strip.
2. Make two copies of the scarecrow, corn, haystack, and cornucopia templates on card stock and color them. Cut them out.
3. Place the title and the first two lines of the poem in the chart.

TEACHING WITH THE POCKET CHART

1. Ask children if they've ever seen a real scarecrow. Some may recall the scarecrow character in *The Wizard of Oz*. Encourage children to describe a scarecrow. Ask, "What is it made of? What does it look like?"
2. Read the title and the first two lines of the poem. Ask, "Who is the scarecrow supposed to scare?" (*Crows and other birds that may feed on crops, such as corn*) "Why do you think there's no one left to scare?"

3. Add the next four lines of the poem and read them aloud. Explain that fall is the time when fruits, vegetables, and other crops are harvested or picked by farmers.

4. Ask, "When do farmers plant what they harvest in the fall?" *(Spring)* Add the last three lines of the poem and read them. Ask, "Why would the scarecrow be scary again in spring?" *(Because that's when birds will return to feed on the plants and seeds. The scarecrow will frighten them away.)*

FOLLOW-UP ACTIVITIES

* Ask children what crops they can think of other than corn that grow in a field.

* Purchase a dried cornstalk from a farmer's market that still has some corn on it. Place an ear in shallow water and watch it start

to sprout in a few days.

* Make small cornhusk dolls with the children. Peel the husks off the corn. Form a ball out of tissue paper and lay it in the middle of a husk. Tie the section with string to form a head. To form an arm, fold another husk in half and tie it near the folded end to make the hand. Repeat to make another arm. Slip the arms under the head, just below the tied part. Tie a string below the arms to form a waist. Divide the husks in half and tie off the ends to form legs. Children can draw faces on the dolls and glue on scraps of cloth and yarn for clothes and hair.

LITERATURE LINKS

Dragonfly's Tale by Kristina Rodanas (Clarion, 1995)

Itse Selu Cherokee Harvest Festival by Daniel Pennington (Charlesbridge, 1994)

Picking Apples and Pumpkins by Amy and Richard Hutchings (Scholastic, 1994)

The Magic Cornfield by Nancy Willard (Harcourt Brace & Co., 1997)

NOVEMBER

WHO'S STUFFED?

PURPOSE

Children discuss their families' and cultures' celebrations and foods.

POCKET CHART POEM

Who's Stuffed?

by Valerie Schiffer

Turkey

Stuffing

Gravy

Corn and squash

Cranberries

And pumpkin pie too.

I'm not sure

Who's really stuffed

The turkey or you!

MATERIALS

* 34- by 42-inch pocket chart
* 10 sentence strips, at least one of each color
* food templates (pages 32–33)
* card stock
* colored markers
* scissors

SETTING UP

1. Write each line of the poem on a different-color sentence strip.
2. Copy the food templates on card stock. Color them, then cut them out.
3. Place the food templates in the chart, as shown on the next page.

TEACHING WITH THE POCKET CHART

1. Invite children to talk about their families' Thanksgiving traditions. Ask, "What do you usually do to celebrate Thanksgiving? What are some of your favorite foods?"
2. Ask the children to name the foods they recognize on the chart. Hold up one of the food words and ask for a volunteer to read the word and match it to the correct food template. Repeat with the other foods.
3. Place the rest of the words in the chart. Read the poem with your class.

FOLLOW-UP ACTIVITIES

* Photocopy the food templates, reducing them in size. Make enough copies so that each child in your class can create his or her own mini-Thanksgiving table. Give each child a set of copies and a piece of 12- by 18-inch paper for a table. Invite children to label the foods and to draw other foods they eat during Thanksgiving.

* Using a 12- by 18-inch piece of paper, have each child create an individual place mat. Be sure they include utensils, a plate, a napkin, and a glass. You can even give each child a paper plate to glue onto his or her paper place mat.

* Use this poem for older children as a springboard to write about the foods on their Thanksgiving table, or a poem called "Thanksgiving is . . ."

* Make a graph that shows the children's favorite Thanksgiving food. Remove the sentence strips from the chart and move the food templates to the left of the chart. Give each child a 3- by 3-inch piece of paper on which to draw his or her own picture. Then invite children to place their picture next to their favorite food in the chart.

LITERATURE LINKS

A Turkey for Thanksgiving by Eve Bunting (Clarion, 1995)

T'was the Night Before Thanksgiving by Dav Pilkey (Orchard Books, 1990)

The Greatest Table by Michael J. Rosen (Harcourt Brace & Co., 1994)

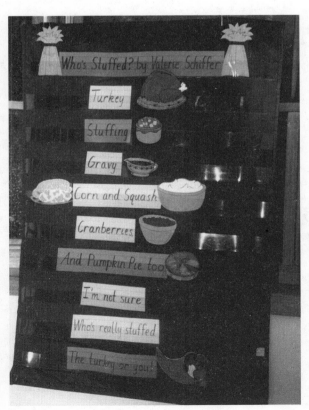

SCARECROW'S HARVEST TEMPLATES

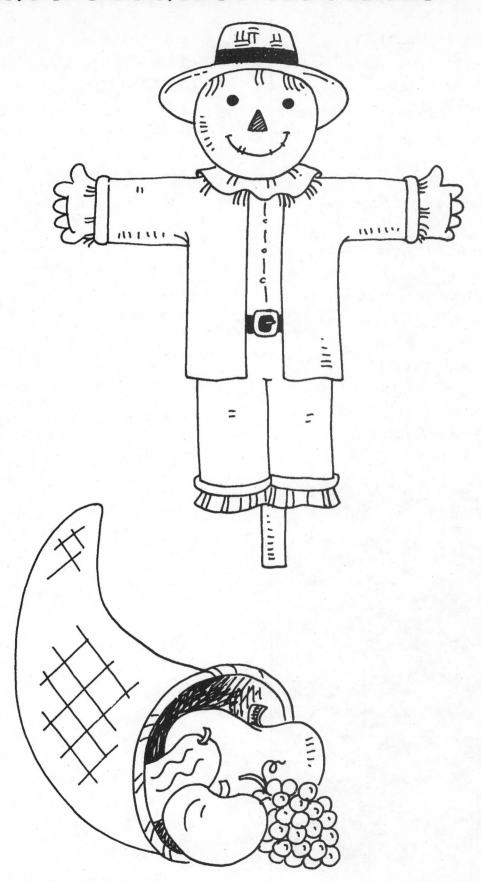

SCARECROW'S HARVEST TEMPLATES

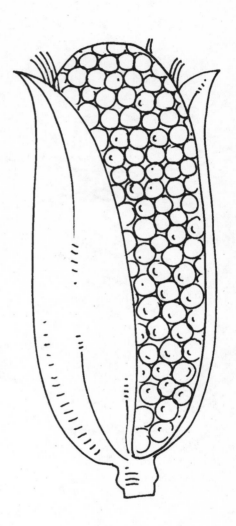

WHO'S STUFFED? TEMPLATES

WHO'S STUFFED? TEMPLATES

DECEMBER

Brighten up your classroom with poems and activities
that celebrate the winter holidays*.

HANUKKAH RAINBOW

PURPOSE

Children learn about and celebrate the
cultural traditions of the Jewish holiday
of Hanukkah.

POCKET CHART POEM

Hanukkah Rainbow

by Eva Grant

Eight little candles in a row,

Gaily colored,

All aglow.

Scarlet, purple,

Green, white, blue,

Pink and yellow,

Orange too.

The menorah,

Shining bright,

Holds a rainbow

Hanukkah night.

*Editor's note: Hanukkah and Christmas are perhaps the
most commercially recognized celebrations at this time of
year. See the Follow-Up Activities for other holidays that
you can introduce to your class.

MATERIALS

* 34- by 42-inch pocket chart
* 9 white sentence strips
* 1 sentence strip each of red, purple, green,
  blue, pink, yellow, and orange
* menorah and candle templates (page 39)
* self-adhesive Velcro
* easel clips
* card stock
* colored markers
* scissors

SETTING UP

1. Copy the color words in the poem on
same-color sentence strips. Write the rest
of the poem on white sentence strips.

2. Copy the menorah and nine candles on
card stock. (The ninth candle, which
sits in the center holder, is called the
shamash, and is used to light the other
candles.) Color the other candles to
match the colors in the poem.

3. Evenly space the hook side of the small
Velcro pieces along the top of the menorah. Place the loop side of the Velcro
pieces on the bottom of each candle so
you can easily attach each candle to the
menorah.

4. Slip sentence strips in the pockets and clip the menorah to the chart.

5. You may want to bring in other Hanukkah symbols, such as a dreidel or even a real menorah and candles. (Because lit candles pose an obvious hazard in the classroom, you may want to get an electric menorah instead.)

TEACHING WITH THE POCKET CHART

1. Find out if any children in your class celebrate Hanukkah. Encourage them to talk about their holiday—what it means and what they do to celebrate it. Be sure to allow for questions and answers.

2. Explain that Hanukkah is a Jewish holiday that celebrates a miracle that happened more than 2,000 years ago. A jar of oil, enough to burn for only one day, was found among the ruins of the Temple of Jerusalem. During the rededication of the temple, the oil miraculously burned for eight days and nights. Every year, Jewish families around the world celebrate Hanukkah by lighting the menorah for eight days. You may want to add that long ago, people burned wicks in oil rather than candles.

3. Read the entire poem to the children. Ask for volunteers to put a matching-color candle on the menorah as you read each color aloud.

FOLLOW-UP ACTIVITIES

* To reinforce the holiday in your class, you may want to add a candle to the menorah for each of the eight days of Hanukkah. The shamash is an additional candle used to light the others. It is always lit first and usually stays in the middle of the menorah each night.

* Invite a parent to share the celebration with your class by bringing in potato pancakes (latkes) and applesauce for a festive snack. Ask a parent to join your class and teach the dreidel game.

* Introduce children to the African-American celebration of Kwanzaa. The word Kwanzaa is Swahili for "first fruits." Kwanzaa begins on December 26 and lasts for seven days until January 1. During this holiday, seven candles are set on a *kinara*, a candleholder usually carved of wood. The seven candles represent the principles

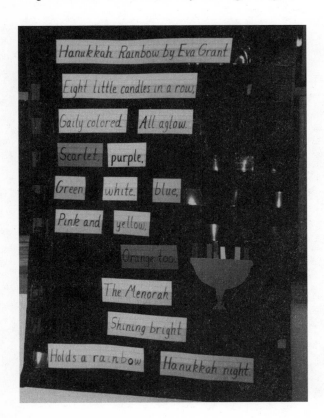

of African-American culture: unity, self-determination, collective work and responsibility, cooperative economics, purpose, creativity, and faith. Family members light one of the seven candles each night and discuss the principle of the day. Then they exchange presents, which are usually homemade.

* Write the following poem on sentence strips to put on your pocket chart:

Kwanzaa by Valerie Schiffer
Seven candles
All aglow
In the kinara
Help us know
Our roots
Our values
Our customs
And long ago.

Cut a kinara from brown tagboard to resemble wood. Trace and cut one black candle, three red candles, and three green candles. Attach the candles to the kinara using Velcro and clip the kinara to the chart.

LITERATURE LINKS
Celebrations of Light by Nancy Luenn (Atheneum, 1998)

Hershel and the Hanukkah Goblins by Eric Kimmel (Holiday House, 1994)

The Chanukkah Guest by Eric Kimmel (Holiday House, 1992)

Hanukkah! by Roni Schotter (Little Brown, 1993)

My First Kwanzaa by Deborah Newton Chocolate (Scholastic, 1992)

It's Kwanzaa Time by Linda and Clay Goss (Philomel, 1995)

DECEMBER

TRIM A TREE

PURPOSE

Children use patterning and counting skills to decorate a Christmas tree.

POCKET CHART POEM

> Trim a Tree
>
> Trim our little tree.
>
> Make a pattern for you and me.
>
> Use 4 snowmen, 4 mittens,
>
> 4 gingerbread boys, and 4 bulbs.

MATERIALS

* 24- by 24-inch pocket chart
* 7 red and green sentence strips
* 22- by 28-inch piece of green tagboard
* small piece of brown tagboard
* tree and decoration templates (pages 40–41)
* self-adhesive Velcro
* card stock
* colored markers
* scissors
* glue
* easel clips

SETTING UP

1. Write the poem on alternating red and green sentence strips. Place the sentence strips on the chart.

2. Make an enlarged photocopy of the tree template. Trace the copy onto green and brown tagboard. Cut out the tree and glue the leaves and trunk together. Clip the tree to the chart below the poem.

3. Cut small pieces of Velcro and stick the hook side on the tree in rows, as shown in the photograph on the next page.

4. Make four copies of each ornament on card stock and color them. Cut them out. Attach the loop side of the Velcro pieces on the back of each ornament.

5. Place the ornaments next to their names on the poem.

TEACHING WITH THE POCKET CHART

1. Find out how many children decorate a tree for Christmas. Invite them to describe what they do and how they decorate the tree. Then tell the children that you have a tree in the classroom to decorate.

2. Read the poem to or with your class. Show them how to place the ornaments on the tree.

3. Create a simple pattern using the ornaments. For example, put the following ornaments in order: snowman, mitten,

gingerbread boy, ball, snowman, and mitten. Ask for a volunteer to come up and place the next ornament in the pattern. Continue until all the ornaments have been put up on the tree. Once the tree is decorated, count the number of ornaments.

4. Invite children to make their own patterns on the tree. They can challenge classmates to continue the pattern until all ornaments have been hung. Older children can see how many variations of patterns can be made using the same number of ornaments.

Note: You can use this activity for your math lessons or as an individual activity.

FOLLOW-UP ACTIVITIES

* Photocopy the tree and ornament templates, reducing them in size. Give these to children so they can create their own patterns.
* Take a field trip to look at decorated trees.
* Introduce children to the Mexican Christmas celebration of Las Posadas, which is held every night during the nine days before Christmas. During Las Posadas, participants reenact Joseph and Mary's search for a place to stay before the birth of Jesus. A group of people carrying candles walk through town, knocking on doors and asking if there's room at the inn. The first two houses refuse them, but the third house invites the group inside for a party.

LITERATURE LINKS
The Trees of the Dancing Goats by Patricia Polacco (Aladdin, 2000)

Tree of Cranes by Allen Say (Houghton Mifflin, 1991)

The Little Fir Tree by Margaret Wise Brown (HarperCollins, 1979)

HANUKKAH RAINBOW TEMPLATES

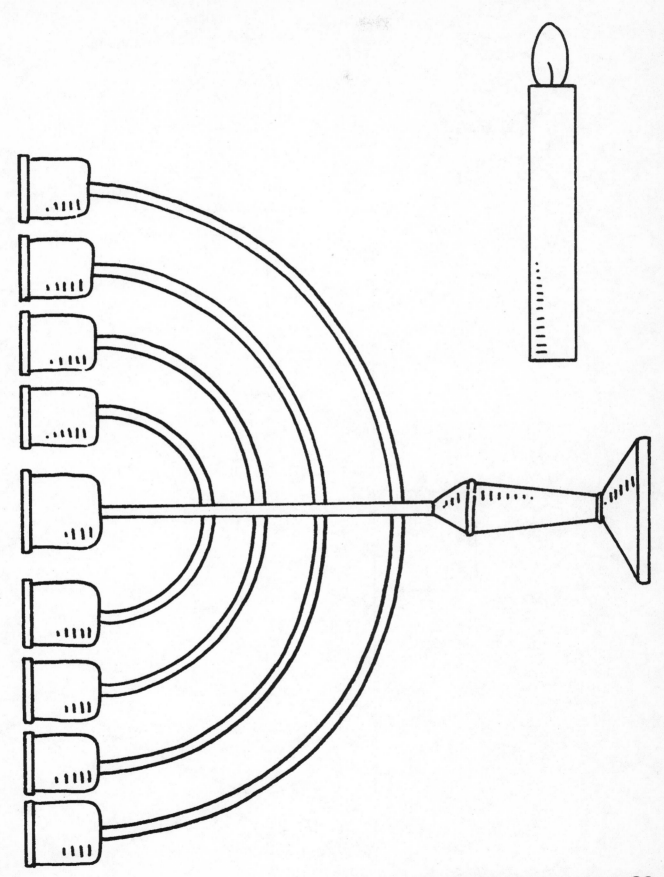

TRIM A TREE TEMPLATES

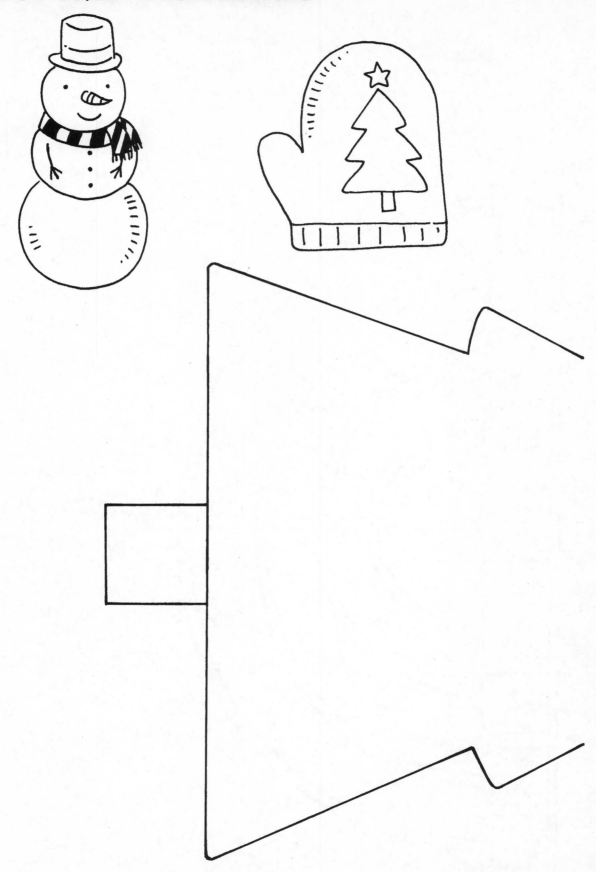

TRIM A TREE TEMPLATES

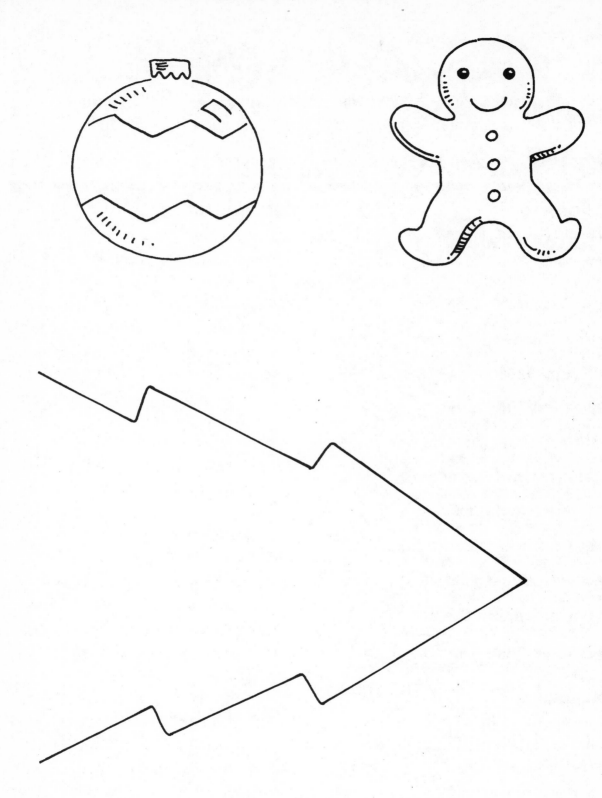

JANUARY

Celebrate the Chinese New Year to add a warm glow to your classroom.
Welcome winter with a whimsical poem about a snow family.

HAPPY CHINESE NEW YEAR

PURPOSE

Children learn about and celebrate the Chinese New Year.

POCKET CHART POEM

Happy Chinese New Year

by Helen H. Moore

"Gung Hay Fat Choy!"

In China, every girl and boy

celebrates the New Year

in a very special way—

With fireworks and dragons,

colored red and gold—

They welcome in the new year

and chase away the old!

MATERIALS

* 34- by 42-inch pocket chart
* 9 white sentence strips
* red and black markers
* dragon and children templates
  (pages 46–47)
* scissors   * card stock

SETTING UP

1. Write each line of the poem on a separate sentence strip, alternating with black and red markers for each line.
2. Copy the dragon and children templates on card stock. Color them, then cut them out. The dragon templates are designed to connect like a jigsaw puzzle. You can use as many pieces in the middle as you like. See the Follow-Up Activities for more ideas.
3. Place the poem and dragon templates in the pocket chart.

TEACHING WITH THE POCKET CHART

1. Before introducing the pocket chart poem to children, you may first want to read a book about the Chinese New Year. (See Literature Links, page 43.) Engage children in a discussion about how they celebrate New Year at home.
2. Explain that the Chinese New Year is a spring festival that was first celebrated more than 5,000 years ago. Celebrations include fireworks, a parade, and gift giving. The date for the Chinese New Year is determined by the lunar calendar, which

follows the cycles of the moon and changes from year to year. The Chinese New Year usually falls between the second week of January and the middle of February.

3. Read the poem with your class. Discuss the meaning of *new* and *old*.

FOLLOW-UP ACTIVITIES

* Photocopy a dragon part for each child in your class. Invite each child to design and color the dragon part to represent himself or herself. Have the children write their names on their dragon part. Cut out the individual pieces and glue them together onto one large piece of tagboard to create a class display. Write "Gung Hay Fat Choy!" on the completed dragon to wish everyone a Happy New Year.

* Local Chinese restaurants usually offer special menus at this time of year. Order some dishes for your class to share, or visit a nearby Chinese restaurant for a luncheon field trip. If you live in or near a large city, there may be a "Chinatown" where you can take your students to visit to learn more about Chinese culture and trade.

* Invite a person of Chinese heritage into your classroom to share stories about his or her culture.

* The Chinese Lunar Calendar has a 12-year cycle, with each year named after an animal. In order, the animals are Rat (1996), Ox (1997), Tiger (1998), Rabbit (1999), Dragon (2000), Snake (2001), Horse (2002), Sheep (2003), Monkey (2004), Rooster (2005), Dog (2006), and Boar (2007). List the animals and the years they represent in a chart. Then help children figure out what animal represents the year they were born. For example, if some of your students were born in 1995, they were born in the Year of the Boar. You can extend this math activity for older children and challenge them to follow the pattern and generate a list of the animals from 1980 to 2020.

LITERATURE LINKS

Sam and the Lucky Money by Karen Chinn (Lee & Low Books, 1997)

Chinese New Year by Tricia Brown (Henry Holt, 1997)

Lion Dancer: Ernie Wan's Chinese New Year by Kate Waters and Madeline Slovenz-Low (Scholastic, 1991)

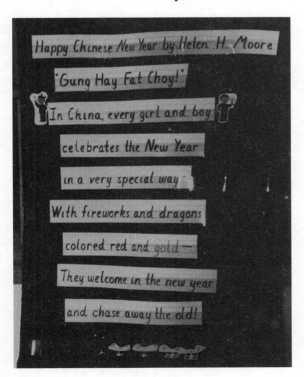

JANUARY

SNOWMAN FAMILY

PURPOSE
Children learn about comparative size and the properties of snow.

POCKET CHART POEM

Snowman Family

by Valerie Schiffer

It snowed last night.

And I can see

The big snowman

And family

Under the tree.

Who made them so?

I do not know.

But three are here

Each time there's snow.

MATERIALS
* 34- by 42-inch pocket chart
* 10 white sentence strips
* snow family templates (page 48)
* white paper
* colored markers
* card stock   * scissors

SETTING UP
1. Write each line of the poem on a separate sentence strip.
2. Copy the snow family on card stock. Color and cut out each snowman.
3. Place the poem and snow family in the chart.
4. Make paper snowflakes and place them in the chart as well. (See instructions under the Follow-Up Activities.)

TEACHING WITH THE POCKET CHART
1. Explain to children where snow comes from. They probably know that snow falls from clouds, just like rain. Explain that when temperatures are freezing cold, tiny ice crystals form in the clouds. The ice crystals join to form snowflakes as they fall from the clouds. If the air temperature near the ground is freezing, the snowflakes continue to fall as snow. If the temperature is warmer, the snowflakes melt and fall as rain.
2. Ask, "What do you like to do when it snows?"
3. Read the poem with children. Ask, "Why do you suppose there's a snow family every time it snows? Do you think someone may have built the snow people, or

did the snow cover some things that were already there? What things might look like snow people when they are covered with snow?"

4. Direct the children's attention to the snow family and each member's size. Encourage them to speculate on who each member might be. Call on a volunteer to point to the biggest snowman. Ask, "Who do you think is the biggest member of the snow family?" *(Some may say the father.)* Have someone else point to the smallest family member. Ask, "Who do you think is the smallest one?" *(Some may say the child or the baby of the family.)* Ask, "What about the medium one? Why do you think so?"

FOLLOW-UP ACTIVITIES

* Create a winter wonderland right in your classroom. Give children white paper circles. Have them fold the circles in half,

then in half again. Have them snip off small pieces along the edges and around the tips. Make sure children don't cut apart the paper. When children unfold their papers, they will look like snowflakes.

* Invite children to describe how they would make a snowman. You can have older children write a step-by-step process, including the size of the snowballs they use.

* Give children three different-size circles. Have them glue these together to create a paper snowman. Provide them with craft materials, such as buttons and colored construction paper, to decorate their snowman.

* Take a snowy-day walk with your class. Challenge children to guess the objects that may be covered with snow.

* If possible, build a real snowman outside with your class. Encourage children to keep a class journal and record daily changes to the snowman.

LITERATURE LINKS

Snow is Falling by Franklyn M. Branley (HarperCollins, 2000)

The Biggest Best Snowman by Margery Cuyler (Scholastic, 1998)

Wintertime by Ann Schweninger (Puffin, 1993)

The Snowy Day by Ezra Jack Keats (Viking Press, 1981)

HAPPY CHINESE NEW YEAR TEMPLATES

HAPPY CHINESE NEW YEAR TEMPLATES

SNOWMAN FAMILY TEMPLATES

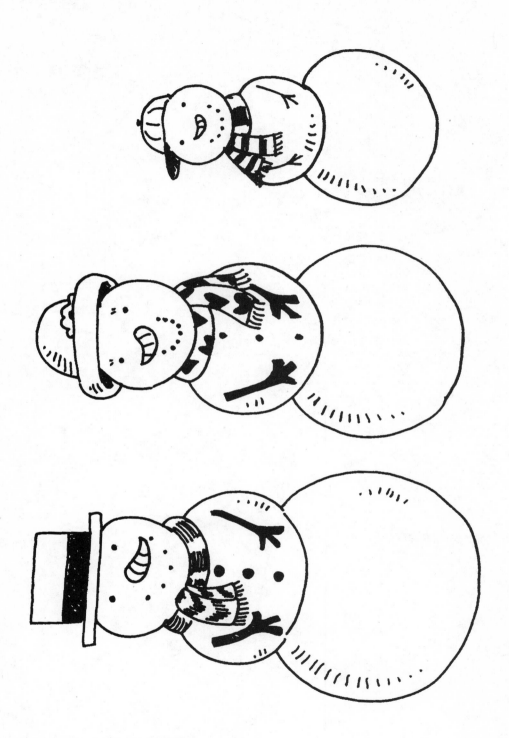

FEBRUARY

This month brings the 100th Day in many schools.
And as always, children can count on a lot of love on Valentine's Day.

TEN TENS TRAIL MIX

POCKET CHART WORDS

Ten Tens Trail Mix

Count to ten, then count again

until you have ten tens

in your zip-lock bag.

10 sunflower seeds

10 raisins

10 chocolate chips

10 pretzels

10 peanut-butter chips

10 apple pieces

10 pieces of popcorn

10 banana chips

10 pumpkin seeds

10 walnuts

Zip your bag tight!

Shake and eat!

PURPOSE

Children practice counting to ten and skip counting to 100. Older children will understand that 10 sets of 10s equal 100.

MATERIALS

* 34- by 42-inch pocket chart
* 10 sentence strips of various colors
* food templates (pages 54–56)
* colored markers
* card stock
* scissors
* chocolate chips, peanut-butter chips, apple pieces, popcorn, small pretzels, banana chips, pumpkin seeds, walnuts, raisins, sunflower seeds or other small snack foods
* 10 large bowls and spoons
* sandwich bags (one for each child in your class)

SETTING UP

1. Write each line of the poem on a separate sentence strip.
2. Copy the food templates on card stock. Color the templates and cut them out. Then, place them in a sandwich bag.
3. Place the sentence strips in the pocket chart.

4. Set up the real food in separate bowls with spoons. Arrange the bowls on a table, buffet style. This way, children can walk up in turn to count the food into their bags.

TEACHING WITH THE POCKET CHART

1. Explain to your class that you are making a special snack to celebrate the 100th Day of School.

2. Read the pocket chart directions with the children. Show them the sandwich bag containing the food templates. As you reread the directions on the chart, call on a volunteer to find the food template in the bag that matches the food word you

just read. Call on a different child for each food.

3. When all the food templates are in place, read the poem again with the class. Invite children to count with you from one to ten.

4. Ask children, "If you have 10 pieces of each kind of food, and there are 10 kinds of food, how many pieces of food do you have in all?" *(100)* To help children understand that 10 sets of 10 equal 100, have them help you count by tens as you point to each food template in turn.

5. Hand a sandwich bag to each child and explain that they will fill their bag with 10 pieces of each food on the table. If necessary, practice counting to 10 again with the children.

6. Have children form a line in front of the buffet table and fill their bags in turn with 10 pieces of each food. You can reinforce the concept of 10 sets of 10 by having them count all the food pieces in their bag. Then invite the children to eat their yummy snacks together.

FOLLOW-UP ACTIVITIES

* Encourage children to group different objects (for example, pennies, crayons, pencils, etc.) by 10s.

* For younger children, you may want to have them make smaller groups of objects, such as by twos or fives.

* Challenge older children to find other ways of grouping 100 math manipulatives. For example, they could create five sets of 20 or two sets of 50.
* Make a 100th Day collaborative book. Divide your class into 10 groups. Have each group illustrate a set of 10 objects on a piece of paper. Encourage them to draw objects that remind them of the first 100 days of school. Then put the pages together to make the 100th Day book.

LITERATURE LINKS

One Smiling Grandma by Ann Marie Linden (Puffin, 1995)

One Hundred is a Family by Pam Munoz Ryan (Hyperion Book for Young Children, 1994)

From One to One Hundred by Teri Sloat (Puffin, 1995)

FEBRUARY

FIVE PRETTY VALENTINES

POCKET CHART POEM

Five pretty valentines waiting
in a store.

_____ bought one and then
there were four.

Four pretty valentines shaped
just like a "V."

_____ bought one and then
there were three.

Three pretty valentines said,
"I love you."

_____ bought one and then
there were two.

Two pretty valentines—this was
so much fun!

_____ bought one and then
there was one.

One pretty valentine sitting
on the shelf.

I felt sorry for it, so I bought it
for myself.

PURPOSE

Children celebrate Valentine's Day as they practice subtraction.

MATERIALS

* 34- by 42-inch pocket chart
* 10 pink sentence strips
* white sentence strips
* 4-inch white heart doilies (one for each child in your class)
* 6-inch red heart doilies (one for each child in your class)
* red and black markers
* valentine stickers (optional)

SETTING UP

1. Write each line of the poem on a separate sentence strip.
2. Write each child's name on a white sentence strip using a red marker. Decorate the name strips with heart stickers.
3. Make a valentine for each child in your class by gluing a 4-inch white doily onto a 6-inch red heart doily. Write each child's name in the center of each white doily.
4. Use a blank sentence strip to cover *four, three, two,* and *one* on the second, fourth, sixth, and eighth sentences, respectively.

5. Display this poem about one week before Valentine's Day. Alternate the children's names so that each child will see his or her name on the chart once.

TEACHING WITH THE POCKET CHART

1. Hold up five valentines in your hand. Make sure the names on the valentines match the names of the children on the chart.

2. Read the first two lines of the poem. As you read the child's name in the second line, hand him or her a valentine. Pause before the covered word on the strip, giving the children time to call out the correct number. When they say "four," remove the blank strip to reveal the number.

3. Continue reading the rest of the poem, repeating the procedure in step 2. When you reach the end of the poem, ask the children, "How many valentines are left?" *(None)*

4. Repeat the poem each day until everyone in your class has had his or her name on the chart.

FOLLOW-UP ACTIVITIES

* Encourage the children in your class to make valentines for each other or for their friends or family.

* Invite children to make valentines for a local hospital or a retirement home.

* Have young children continue to practice subtracting by ones using math manipulatives.

LITERATURE LINKS

Four Valentines in a Rainstorm by Felicia Bond (HarperFestival, 1999)

Valentine's Day by Gail Gibbons (Holiday House, 1986)

A Book of Hugs by Dave Ross (HarperTrophy, 2000)

TEN TENS TRAIL MIX TEMPLATES

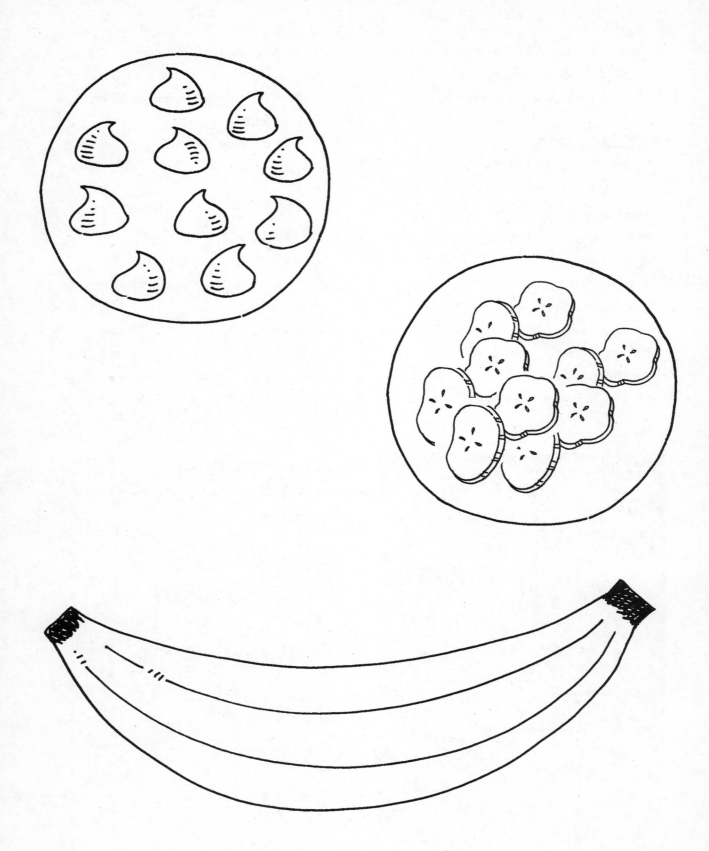

TEN TENS TRAIL MIX TEMPLATES

TEN TENS TRAIL MIX TEMPLATES

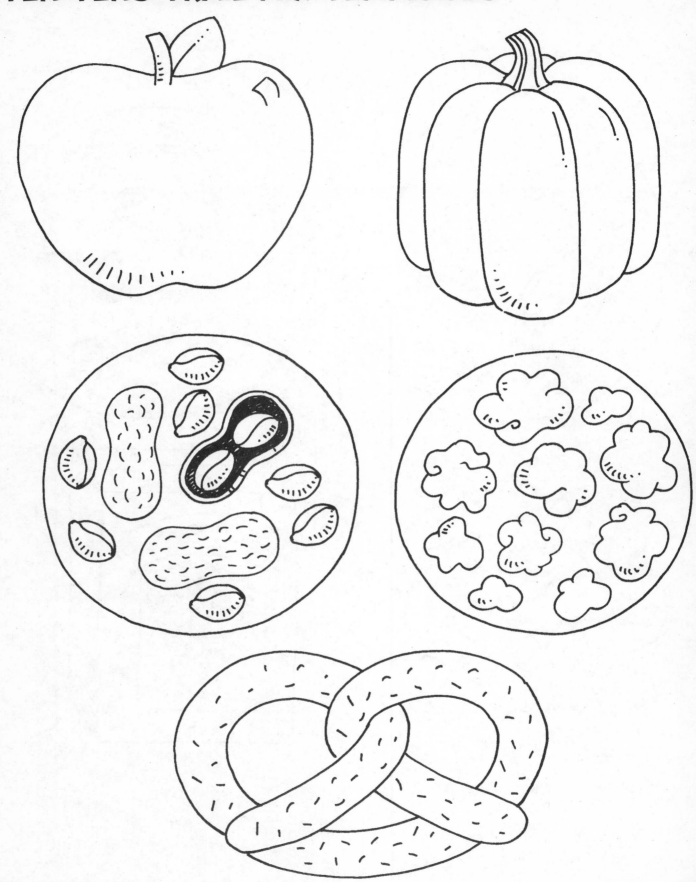

MARCH

As March winds blow, let children's fancies soar as they imagine themselves riding the breeze. Hunt for a lucky four-leaf clover this spring.

A KITE

PURPOSE

Children explore the properties of air and wind, and use their imaginations.

POCKET CHART POEM

A Kite

I often sit and wish that I

Could be a kite up in the sky

And ride upon the breeze and go

Whichever way I chanced to blow.

MATERIALS

* 24- by 24-inch pocket chart
* 5 sentence strips (2 in one color, 2 in another, and 1 white)
* kite and boy templates (page 61)
* colored markers
* card stock
* scissors

SETTING UP

1. Write each line of the poem on a separate sentence strip. If possible, emphasize the rhyming lines by writing them on the same-color strips.

2. Copy the kite and boy templates on card stock. Color the templates and cut them out.

3. Place the sentence strips and templates in the chart.

TEACHING WITH THE POCKET CHART

1. Ask your class if anyone has ever felt himself or herself being pushed by a strong wind. What does it feel like? Explain to children that the wind is just moving air.

2. Read the poem with your class.

3. Invite the children to close their eyes and imagine how it feels to soar in the sky as the wind blows them here and there.

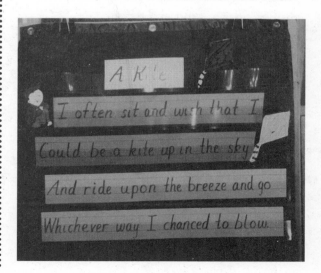

Ask, "What else do you see the wind blow around?"

FOLLOW-UP ACTIVITIES

* Enlarge the kite template and invite each child to design his or her own kite. Display the kites in the classroom to celebrate windy March.

* The Beaufort scale measures wind strength based on its effects on objects. For example, in a light breeze, leaves rustle. A moderate breeze blows paper around, while a strong breeze makes it difficult for a person to hold an umbrella. Invite children to observe the effects of wind outside and create their own scale of wind strength.

* Collect a variety of metal objects, such as keys, nails, screws, and spoons. Invite children to make wind chimes by poking holes along the rim of a paper cup and tying the metal objects to the cup, using 6-inch long pieces of yarn. Hang the wind chimes near a window or door.

* Have older children do research to find out more about stronger, more destructive winds associated with tornadoes and hurricanes.

LITERATURE LINKS

Wind by Ron Bacon
(Scholastic, 1993)

Catch the Wind! by Gail Gibbons
(Little Brown, 1989)

How the Wind Plays by Michael Lipson
(Hyperion, 1994)

The Emperor and the Kite by Jane Yolen
(Paperstar, 1998)

MARCH

FIND A CLOVER

PURPOSE
Children will understand the math concept of probability.

POCKET CHART POEM

Find a Clover by Valerie Schiffer

I'm looking all over

For a four-leaf clover.

If just one I could see

How lucky I would be!

MATERIALS
* 24- by 24-inch pocket chart
* 4 green sentence strips
* leprechaun, three-leaf clover, and four-leaf clover templates (page 61)
* colored markers (including dark and light green)
* card stock
* scissors
* paper bag

SETTING UP
1. Write each line of the poem on a separate sentence strip.
2. Make one copy each of the leprechaun and the four-leaf clover, and six copies of the three-leaf clovers on card stock.

Color three three-leaf clovers light green, and the rest, including the four-leaf clover, dark green. Color the leprechaun as well. Cut them all out.
3. Place the poem and clover in the chart.

TEACHING WITH THE POCKET CHART
1. Read the poem to your class.
2. Ask if they have ever seen a four-leaf clover. Explain that most clovers have only three leaves, so some people believe that finding one with four leaves brings luck. Ask, "What do you think are your chances of finding a four-leaf clover?"
3. Explain that chances have to do with probability. Take all the clovers from the chart, put them in the paper bag, and shake the bag. Ask, "What are the chances of pulling out the four-leaf clover?" Call on a volunteer to come and pick a clover out of the bag. Is it the four-leaf clover? Repeat the procedure 10 times, calling on a different volunteer each time. How many times did the four-leaf clover come up?
4. Ask, "Which do you think would be easier to pick out of the bag—a four-leaf clover or a light-green clover?" Remind children that three out of seven clovers are light green, while only one out of

seven is a four-leaf clover. Repeat the experiment in step 3. How many times did the four-leaf clover come up? How many times did a light-green clover come up?

FOLLOW-UP ACTIVITIES

* Copy, color, and cut out more clovers. Add them to those already in the bag and repeat the experiment in step 3 of "Teaching With the Pocket Chart." Have children keep track on paper of how many times you draw a dark-green or light-green clover.

* Give each child a paper cup half-filled with soil and a few clover seeds. When the seeds sprout and grow, have children look for four-leaf clovers in their cups.

* Encourage children to play with dice to further understand the concept of probability. Have them roll a die several times and record how many times each number comes up.

LITERATURE LINKS

Spring: A Haiku Story selected by George Shannon (William Morrow, 1996)

Jamie O'Rourke and the Big Potato: An Irish Folk Tale by Tomie dePaola (Paperstar, 1997)

A KITE AND FIND A CLOVER TEMPLATES

APRIL

This month brings showers that revive the earth.
Help children reflect on ways they can help save the planet.

SUDDEN STORM

PURPOSE

Children recognize rhymes and discuss metaphors.

POCKET CHART POEM

Sudden Storm

by Elizabeth Coatsworth

The rain comes in sheets

Sweeping the streets,

Here, here, and here,

Umbrellas appear.

Red, blue, yellow, green,

They tilt and they lean

Like mushrooms, like flowers

That grow when it showers.

MATERIALS

* 34- by 42-inch pocket chart
* 12 sentence strips (including red or pink, blue, yellow, and green)
* umbrella, mushroom, and flower templates (page 66)

* colored markers
* card stock
* scissors

SETTING UP

1. Write the color words on coordinating color strips. Copy the rest of the poem on separate sentence strips. If possible, emphasize the rhyming lines by writing them on the same color strips.
2. Copy the templates on card stock. Color them and cut them out.
3. Place the poem and templates in the chart.

TEACHING WITH THE POCKET CHART

1. This is a great poem to put up on a rainy day—the mood has already been set. Children may come into school with rain gear. Introduce the poem by talking about their umbrellas, raincoats, and boots.
2. If you cannot wait for the weather to cooperate, ask children to describe what they wear and use on a rainy day. Read the poem with your class.
3. Reread the last three lines of the poem. Ask, "What do you think the author

means when she says, 'They tilt and they lean like mushrooms, like flowers that grow when it showers'? Why do you think the author used mushrooms and flowers to describe umbrellas?" *(They look alike—an umbrella has a handle that looks like the stem of a mushroom or flower; the top looks like a mushroom cap or the open petals of a flower.)* Explain to children that a *metaphor* is a way of comparing and describing things that are alike.

4. Read the poem again and ask the children to point out words that rhyme. Draw four columns on the board or on chart paper and list the rhyming pairs in each column. Challenge the children to come up with more rhyming words that belong in each column.

FOLLOW-UP ACTIVITIES

* Copy the umbrella templates for younger children. Have them write sets of rhyming words on the umbrella and raincoats. Then glue the templates onto mural paper and entitle it *Rainy Day Rhymes*.

* When children come to school in rain gear, graph the colors of their raincoats.

* When it rains, collect rainwater in jars. Have the children use it with watercolor paints.

* Plant some flower seeds in paper cups or small clay pots. They may bloom for May.

LITERATURE LINKS

Mushroom in the Rain by Mirra Ginsburg (Aladdin, 1997)

Umbrella by Taro Yashima (Penguin, 1986)

Rain Talk by Mary Serfozo (Macmillan, 1990)

APRIL

HAPPY EARTHLINGS

PURPOSE

Children celebrate our planet and explore the meaning of Earth Day.

POCKET CHART POEM

> Happy Earthlings
>
> by Valerie Schiffer
>
> I'm so happy in every way
>
> That I can walk the earth today.
>
> The flowers blooming and the trees,
>
> The rabbits hopping and the bees,
>
> We all really need the same thing—
>
> A cleaner place for all earthlings.

MATERIALS

* 34- by 42-inch pocket chart
* 7 sentence strips in various colors
* Earth, tree, flower, bee, rabbit, and girl templates (pages 67–69)
* colored markers
* card stock
* scissors

SETTING UP

1. Write each line of the poem on a separate sentence strip.
2. Copy the templates on card stock. Color them and cut them out.
3. Place the poem and templates in the chart.

TEACHING WITH THE POCKET CHART

1. Explain to your class that Earth Day is the day in which we celebrate the Earth and think about ways to preserve it. Ask, "What are some ways we can do to save the Earth?" *(Clean up litter, conserve water and electricity, plant trees, etc.)*
2. Encourage the children to talk about what they really appreciate about the Earth, such as wildlife, clean water, forests, and mountains.
3. Tell the children that this poem is about the everyday things we see. Read the poem.
4. Read the poem again and invite children to act out the lines. For example, they could hop like a rabbit, bloom like a flower, buzz like a bee, etc. Children will enjoy taking turns reading and acting out the poem.

FOLLOW-UP ACTIVITIES

* Make a list of the things we need to live, such as clean water, sunlight, fresh air, a place to make a home.
* Celebrate Earth Day in school. Organize an outdoor clean up.
* Take children on a field trip to a local recycling plant.
* Ask older children to write a story about a new baby Earth that they need to care for. What would they need to do to protect it and make sure it grows into a healthy, big Earth?

LITERATURE LINKS

Hey! Get Off Our Train by John Burningham (Crown, 1999)

For the Love of Our Earth by P. K. Hallinan (Ideals Publishing, 1992)

The Great Trash Bash by Loreen Leedy (Holiday House, 2000)

Dear Children of the Earth: A Letter from Home by Schim Schimmel (Northwood Press, 1994)

SUDDEN STORM TEMPLATES

HAPPY EARTHLINGS TEMPLATE

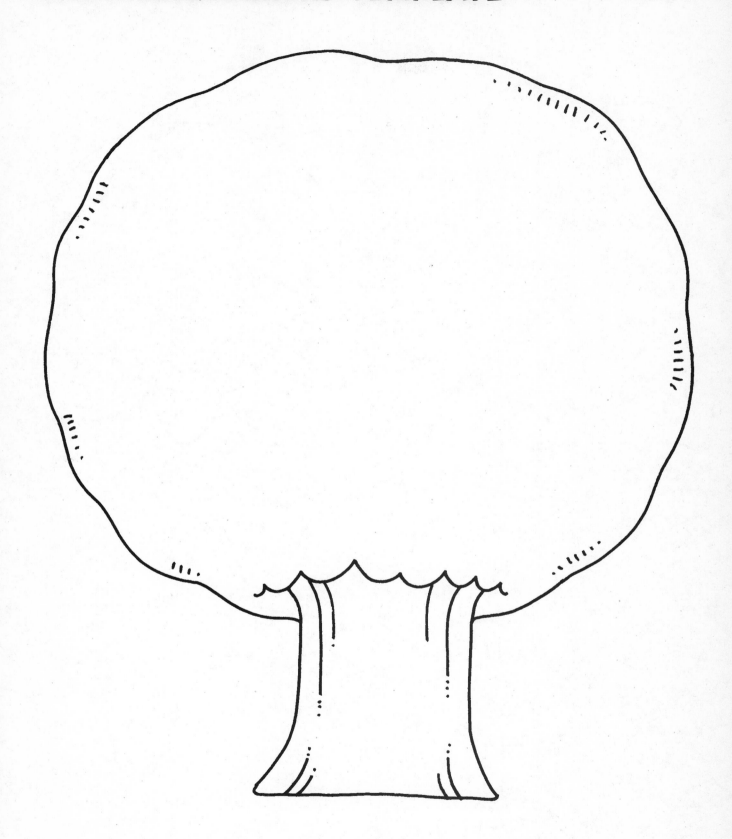

HAPPY EARTHLINGS TEMPLATES

HAPPY EARTHLINGS TEMPLATES

MAY

What's hatching? All sorts of eggs—from chicks to ladybugs.

EGGS ON ME

PURPOSE
Children understand that some animals hatch from eggs.

POCKET CHART POEM

Eggs On Me by Helen H. Moore

Some are big,

some are speckled,

some are brown,

some look freckled.

All have shells,

all must hatch

when the baby inside

goes scritch, scritch, scratch!

Can you guess

what they could be?

Did you say, "Eggs"?

You're right, yessiree!

MATERIALS
* 34- by 42-inch or 42- by 58-inch pocket chart
* 13 sentence strips
* hen and chick templates (page 74)
* colored markers
* card stock
* scissors

SETTING UP
1. Write each line of the poem on a separate sentence strip.
2. Make one copy of the chicken template and four copies of the hatching-egg template on card stock. Color the chicken and the hatching eggs. (You may want to color three eggs according to the poem—one speckled, one brown, and one freckled.) Cut them out, then put them aside.
3. Set up the first 10 lines of the poem on the chart as a riddle. Leave out the title and the last two lines. Give the children a chance to read the clues with you and then guess the answer.

TEACHING WITH THE POCKET CHART

1. Read the poem on the chart with your class. Ask, "Can you guess what the poem is about?" *(Eggs)* When children have guessed correctly, add the title and the last two lines, as well as the templates, on the chart.

2. Read the entire poem again with the children. Ask your class if they know of other animals that hatch from eggs. Make a list on the board or chart paper: for example, snakes, alligators, dinosaurs, and caterpillars. (Older children may be able to classify the animals on the list as reptiles, birds, insects, shellfish, and fish.)

3. Make a second list of animals that are born live. (Don't forget humans!)

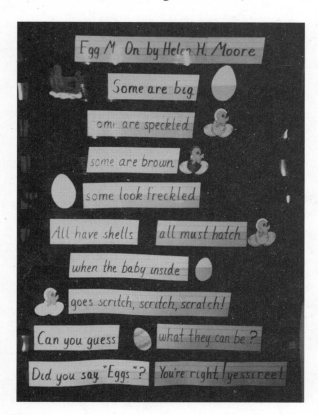

FOLLOW-UP ACTIVITIES

* Make a copy of the hatching egg and cut off the chick. Make several copies of the now-empty egg and have children draw in and color other hatching animals. Then collect all the children's pages to create a collaborative book of animals that hatch from eggs.

* Make up more riddles about animals with your class. Older children can write their own to illustrate and share.

* If feasible, visit a farm to see a hen house. Or, buy an incubator and hatch some fertilized eggs in your classroom.

* Discuss the eggs we eat. Some children may get a little upset by this, so be prepared. Explain that the eggs we buy and eat are not fertilized, and so have no chicks inside them. If no one in the class has any objections, cook eggs for a snack. Talk about the different ways we can cook eggs.

LITERATURE LINKS

The Egg by Gallimard Jeunesse and Pascale de Bourgoing (Scholastic, 1992)

A Nest Full of Eggs by Priscilla Belz Jenkins (HarperCollins, 1995)

Bently & Egg by William Joyce (HarperCollins, 1997)

Rechenka's Eggs by Patricia Polacco (Paperstar, 1996)

Eggbert by Tom Ross (Paperstar, 1997)

MAY

LADYBUGS

PURPOSE

Children learn about ladybugs and how they help in the garden.

POCKET CHART POEM

Ladybugs

by Valerie Schiffer

Ladybugs on the flowers,

Ladybugs on the corn,

Ladybugs on the leaves,

Ladybugs on the lawn.

Ladybugs in my garden

As hungry as can be.

Eating up the aphids,

So something's left for me.

MATERIALS

* 34- by 42-inch pocket chart
* 9 sentence strips
* ladybug, flower, corn, leaf, and child templates (pages 74, 68, 66, 33, and 15)
* colored markers
* card stock
* scissors

SETTING UP

1. Write each line of the poem on a separate sentence strip.
2. Make at least two copies of each template on card stock and color them. Cut them out.
3. Place the sentence strips and templates in the chart. You may want to put aside the flower, leaves, and corn templates to do a word-match exercise with younger children as you recite the poem.

TEACHING WITH THE POCKET CHART

1. Engage children in a discussion about the kinds of insects they can see at this time of year. If some mention ladybugs, have them describe the ladybugs they've seen.
2. Read the poem with the children.
3. Tell children that a ladybug is a kind of insect that is also called a ladybird beetle. Explain that an insect has six legs, three body parts, antennae, and wings. The ladybug has two pairs of wings, although we usually see only

one set—the one that is colored. Explain that not all ladybugs are red; some come in other colors.

4. Discuss how some insects like to eat plants and can be destructive in a garden. For instance, aphids, another kind of insect, can eat through and destroy some plants. Ladybugs love to eat aphids. They even lay their eggs on leaves where aphids live, so that when ladybug larvae hatch, they have a ready meal.

5. Explain that some farmers release ladybugs into their orchards to rid them of destructive aphids. Ladybugs can eat up to 50 aphids a day.

FOLLOW-UP ACTIVITIES

* Copy ladybug templates for children to color. Make a garden mural with ladybugs everywhere. Have children draw or paint

the garden. Then glue on the ladybugs.

* Encourage older children to research other garden helpers or insects.

* If you want to further study ladybugs in the classroom, some science catalogs offer ladybug farms. Ladybugs can be an interesting classroom pet. Have children fill out a daily log of their observations of ladybugs.

* Find out if there's a local gardener who may use ladybugs in his or her garden. See if you can take your class to visit when the gardener releases the ladybugs.

LITERATURE LINKS

The Ladybug and Other Insects by Gallimard Jeunesse and Pascale de Bourgoing (Scholastic, 1991)

The Grouchy Ladybug by Eric Carle (HarperCollins, 1996)

EGGS ON ME AND LADYBUGS TEMPLATES

JUNE

Share the history of our nation's flag with children to celebrate Flag Day. As the school year draws to a close, invite children to think about what summer means to them.

FLAG DAY

PURPOSE

Children learn about the American flag.

POCKET CHART POEM

Flag Day by Valerie Schiffer

June fourteenth's the date

We all celebrate

Our flag that's so great

With stars for each state.

Thirteen stripes fly, too.

Those are there for you.

The first states that flew

Our red, white and blue.

MATERIALS

* 34- by 42-inch pocket chart
* 9 white sentence strips or 3 each of red (or pink), white, and blue
* flag and star templates (pages 79–80)
* red and blue markers
* card stock
* scissors
* an American flag (optional)

SETTING UP

1. Write each line of the poem on a separate sentence strip. If possible, arrange the strips in a red, white, and blue pattern.
2. Copy the flag template on card stock. Color the flag and cut it out.
3. Place the poem and flag in the pocket chart.

TEACHING WITH THE POCKET CHART

1. Use this poem to help you teach the class about our flag. Read the poem to the class.
2. Show the flag and point out the stars and stripes. Invite children to count the stars with you. There are 50 stars, one for each state. Explain that the number of stars has changed over the years as territories joined the union.
3. Have children count the stripes. Explain that even though the number of stars has changed, the 13 stripes have remained the same all throughout. They represent the original British colonies that joined to form the United States. (The extent of your history lesson will depend on the ages of the children in your class.)

4. Have the class read the poem with you.

FOLLOW-UP ACTIVITIES

* Let the children help you cut 50 stars using the template. Use the 50 stars for various math activities.

* Have children carefully observe how the 50 stars are arranged on the flag. Ask, "How else could the stars be arranged in the rectangle? How could it be rearranged if another star were added?" (You may want to use an overhead transparency of the flag for this activity.)

* Challenge older children to research the history of our flag, states, and state flags. You may even have them research flags from other countries.

* Make a copy of the flag for each child. Instruct each child on how to color the flag.

LITERATURE LINKS

Our Flag by Eleanor Ayer (Millbrook, 1994)

If You Lived in Colonial Times by Ann McGovern (Scholastic, 1992)

The Boston Coffee Party by Doreen Rappaport (HarperCollins, 1996)

We the People: The Constitution of the Unites States of America by Peter Spier (Doubleday, 1987)

Our National Holidays by Karen Spies (Millbrook, 1994)

JUNE

JUNE IS A TUNE

PURPOSE
Children celebrate and learn about summer.

POCKET CHART POEM

June Is a Tune by Sarah Wilson

June is a tune

that jumps on a stair.

June is a rose

in a little girl's hair.

June is a bumble

of one small bee.

June is a hug

from the sunshine

to me.

MATERIALS
* 34- by 42-inch pocket chart
* 10 sentence strips
* sun, flower, girl, and bee templates (page 80)
* colored markers
* card stock   * scissors

SETTING UP
1. Write each line of the poem on a separate sentence strip.
2. Copy the templates on card stock. Then color them and cut them out.
3. Place the sentence strips and templates in the pocket chart.

TEACHING WITH THE POCKET CHART
1. Tell the children that summer officially begins around June 21. Explain that the first day of summer is actually the longest day of the year.
2. Read the poem with your class.
3. Engage the children in a discussion about the characteristics of summer. Ask, "What does summer mean to you?" Encourage them to describe summer, especially as related to their senses—the sights, smells, and sounds that remind them of summer. List their descriptions on the board or chart paper.
4. Reread the poem with your class. Invite children to act out parts of the poem, such as the bumblebee, the child climbing stairs, and the warm feeling of the sun.

FOLLOW-UP ACTIVITIES

* Using the list of summer sights and sounds, make a summer mural. Have children draw themselves in the mural. This makes a great end-of-year project to fill those last few days with creative fun.

* Have each child make a mobile of the things they like to do in the summer. Start with a piece of 10- by 12-inch tagboard on which each child writes the word "summer." Punch holes along the bottom edge and tie string from which to hang drawn or cut-out pictures of their favorite summer activities. Help them glue their pictures to tagboard and hang them to their mobiles.

* Invite older children to design a postcard depicting their vacation plans on a 4- by 6-inch index card. Encourage children to exchange addresses with their friends for summer pen pals.

LITERATURE LINKS

The Seasons of Arnold's Apple Tree by Gail Gibbons (Harcourt Brace, Jovanovich, 1984)

Night Letters by Palmyra LoMonaco (Dutton, 1996)

The Little Boat by Kathy Henderson (Candlewick, 1998)

FLAG DAY TEMPLATE

JUNE IS A TUNE TEMPLATES